View from Blue-Jade Mountain

poems by

Robert Merritt

Finishing Line Press
Georgetown, Kentucky

View from Blue-Jade Mountain

for Mimi,
The Voyage of Return

Copyright © 2019 by Robert Merritt
ISBN 978-1-63534-852-1 First Edition
All rights reserved under International and Pan-American Copyright Conventions. No part of this book may be reproduced in any manner whatsoever without written permission from the publisher, except in the case of brief quotations embodied in critical articles and reviews.

ACKNOWLEDGMENTS

"Day after Night on Black Mountain;" "Not Lost: Island Voices" ~ *Kestrel*, Spring 2016
"What Dying College Cannot Take Down with It" ~ *Pine Mountain Sand and Gravel*, 2015
"Book Report;" "Ideogram in Hillsboro, WV;" "Peace Haven Road" ~ *Pikeville Review*, 2017

Publisher: Leah Maines
Editor: Christen Kincaid
Cover Art: Caroline Merritt
Author Photo: Wayne Pelts
Cover Design: Leah Huete

Printed in the USA on acid-free paper.
Order online: www.finishinglinepress.com
also available on amazon.com

Author inquiries and mail orders:
Finishing Line Press
P. O. Box 1626
Georgetown, Kentucky 40324
U. S. A.

Table of Contents

Prelude: Jadelight 1

Nantahalas 2

Peace Haven Road, 2016 3

The Presence of Absence 5

Book Report 8

Alchemy in Hillsboro, WV 11

Returned from China, I Try to Find the Bar We Frequented 14

Houseboat Conjuring 15

Day after Night on Black Mountain 16

What a Dying College Cannot Take Down with It 17

Not Lost: Island Voices 19

International Architects Cycling near Salzburg 21

Brickmaking, Chicago 2016 22

Unwinding the Road 24

Why Don't You Stay, Just a Little Bit Longer? 26

Penelope's Eyes 29

You Live What Birds Know 31

Floating Lanterns 32

Prelude: Jadelight

This book's title, *View from Blue-Jade Mountain*, acknowledges a perspective from the Blue Ridge Mountains where I live, where the blue chicory blooms in spring on hills haunted by a heritage of resources stripped and shipped to illuminate and shelter the lowlands. Jade, which has been called crystalized moonlight, offers a perspective from ancient China's mountains.

I bought a pendent of jade for my wife in Nanjing, China, light green, the most precious. Mimi has lost and found this jade several times. When she was without it, bad luck happened. She now keeps it on her chest, always by her heart.

These mountains up here are fused with the colors of blue and green in summer. Walking along the ridges, I look down to the valleys and think of Li Bai:

>Ask me
>Why I stay
>On Green Mountain
>I smile
>And do not answer.
>My heart is at ease.

I want these poems to answer with help from mountains and the radiating jadelight flowing through the heartbreaks we survive. Jade is the gemstone that diminishes fear. It helps us to remember our dreams. Put it under your pillow. The imagination is jade, with a touch of blue.

(poem translation from *The Heart of Chinese Poetry* by Greg Whincup, Anchor, 1987)

Nantahalas

"Nantahala" (Land of the Noonday Sun): Cherokee Nvda' and aye'li ("sun" and "middle"). "Nvda" can mean eiither sun or moon, so one must specify "nvda iga ehi" (living in the day) or "nvda sunoye ehi" (living in the night).

River, forest,
Nantahala is a way of knowing
how to use the modicum of light
topography offers.

Living for the day in the night.
The sun refuses to shine in hollows
until noon flashes by,
no human watching.

Be grateful for Nantahalas
because a flicker
is enough
to satisfy the advancing shadows.

Return a song
to the land
curling in upon itself
wary and waiting.

Peace Haven Road, 2016

I found Judy at Brookdale, on Peace Haven
Road, with the second-hand information
that she lived at a home for dementia
near Winston-Salem and a desire to
return to the roads of my high school nights.

Last day of May, Judy curled under
bedcovers in running shoes —is she sixty
or eighty?— so, so white that I wanted
to carry her ghost into the sun when
she asked me where my beard came from,
tugging it and saying, "Are you writing? Do you have
any Snickers?" She knew me! I wanted
to give her oranges and pictures of
hummingbirds. What happened to her books?   Her
wonderful marginalia on Han Shan?

Can Judy find peace here, or haven,
on the edge of memory, "out of her mind,"
desiring candy and sunlight?   "I'll walk
you to your car," sensing these visits should
not be prolonged. The manager said, "You
know you can't leave the building now, Judy."
"I want to go outside!" she screamed. They asked
if she wanted a donut. She said "How
'bout moonshine? I want to go outside!" I
was sneaked out a back door and could not hug
or say farewell.

Morning bright and blue, pollen covering
my car. I wanted to go outside. Judy,
never stop demanding sugar and sunlight.

Fifty shot dead in an Orlando nightclub
last night. Oh let there be a peace
someplace where we can cross the threshold
to haven.

Driving away, I finally felt at home
in the place where I was born so determined to escape,
where my parents' ashes remain, and where Judy's
captive alchemy reaffirmed that I had
not refused the call to adventure,
when she insisted upon
sweetness and light on Peace Haven Road.

The Presence of Absence

> *beneath our skins, mountains bulge, rooks flow;*
> *within our chests lurk lost cities, hidden tribes*
> *. . .*
> *follow the path back to its source, else be*
> *a house vacant save for swallows in the eaves.*
> *—Shih-Shu, trans. James Sanford*

Looking out her locked window
at morning sun prisming
through the green leaves
at a home for dementia care
in Winston-Salem,
Judy, pale and lean,
has only her brimming mind for deep company,
a mind which has lost poems about
digging potatoes in Idaho,
the gravel roads of Surry County, N.C.,
a little girl running through red clay dust,
"but I would never want to live there again."

Her poems were curiously uninhabited,
never saying when she was born
or how she ended up in Blacksburg.
I write without uncovering many of my layers,
but she was downright hermetic.

She always made three cups from one tea bag,
and recycled everything,
like all those annotated columns from *The Roanoke Times*
about saving the trees that she mailed to friends;
her main extravagance was stamps,
verifying her community existed.

I go to her little house on Dickinson Lane.
where she lived alone,
with her Boston Terrier,
clothespins on her line in the backyard.
Never using a dryer, she hung jeans in winter to freeze in the sun.

Where are her dog and truck now?

She so cared about surviving without hurting
the earth,
always red clay to her.
A sturdy hoe leans in the garage.

She sharpened her tools
on solitary afternoons.

Did she ever have a husband?
Why did I never ask her?
She just sprang fully formed
from an obscure prairie.
Only a nephew who gives no clues.

Her absence is strong,
her presence keen in the yard
where she fed birds and squirrels
and the sun moves across shadeless windows.

This is what I share with Judy:
a determination to tell,
leaving out essential evidence
our imaginations choose to recycle.

I peer into her dining room window
where I see boxes and imagine
organized folders
with all of the drafts dated.
I want to gather an anthology for her friends.
But to what purpose?
Her writings subsist better
in our minds' meager reconstructions
surrounded by
clothesline, axe handles,
and vacant eaves where swallows nest.

Book Report

I read *The Exile*,
by Pearl Sydenstricker Buck
about her mother, Carie,
about the exile she felt
returning home
to the mountains
of Hillsboro, West Virginia,
every ten years,
an outsider there,
as in China.

That book, out of print,
I found in the library
at the small college
where I teach.

Did the Baptist librarians
in the 1940's know that
after following her husband, Absalom,
through fetid ghettos of China
and watching three children
die in her arms,
Carie hated Saint Paul
and his legacy?

One card in the pocket
of this 1936 library book:
last checked out
by Kay Lawrence, Apr. 1, '74.

The same year that I waited to get out of college,
scared of Viet Nam,
venerating Kerouac on my back porch,
a Baptist girl in the Blue Ridge Mountains
on April Fool's Day
touched a woman's bittersweet
biography of faraway.

Only the faintest pencil
underlinings. Kay
knew not to mark library books:
"beauty was a sort
of oxygen that gave her
life energy."
At a college where
men wore flattops in 1974,
Kay launched her blossoming.

Carie cultivated her "sensuous nature," singing
in the flourishing gardens she made
upon whatever hard plot she found
at the family's evershifting residences.
And Kay? She underlined
"music is not technique and
melody, but the
meaning of life itself, infinitely
sorrowful and unbearably beautiful."
Did Kay become a piano teacher,
or a weaver of tapestries,
or the wife of a missionary?
Underlinings stop on page 67.

Carie went to her heaven,
and her zealous husband to his.

One night in Zhenjiang,
men, angry at foreigners and drought,
came to Carie's house to kill her.
Absalom out, she was ready.
Lights on, doors open,
a party with her children.

She offered tea and
cakes to dark men. Her recipe
for courage was
faith, beauty, hospitality, and
the innocence of children.

The men drank tea,
ate, for they were hungry,
and departed,
axes dragging in the dust.

I open dusty leaves of a book
to sun after 40 years,
feeling Kay feeling Pearl listening
to Carie, singing the wisdom of exile:
— "Who knows, God may like
laughter and dancing and beauty." —
in the restorative air
of discrete mountains.

Alchemy in Hillsboro, WV

Pearl Buck's birthplace,
rainstorm on July afternoon,
plateau flashing green
where industrious Dutch
had faced that wilderness stouthearted,
cleared shadows,
and crafted
dependable houses, clocks.

Because I had been to Pearl's little house in Nanjing,
and felt Han Shan present in these mountains,
I have been asked
to make a few remarks
on her 132nd birthday.
Puddles in tractor ruts,
tents sagging and dripping
while her Chinese cloaks hang
dry in the columned house
solidly built
by those Dutch watchmakers.

"Sh'i," the ideogram for poetry,
means speech for the holy place,
the strokes pointing out how to feel at home anywhere.
Pearl carried this place,
to China.

Today, China far away,
a family singing gospel on the cabin porch,
birthday cake and punch waiting,
and rainfall,
make another ideogram,
a hallowed speaking place
ripe for transformation.

My ego ablaze in this village,
as the first step in alchemy is calcination.
Burn and purify some common element
in a crucible
to just before ash.

"Just one glimpse of Him in gloryland
Will the toils of life repay,"
sings the gospel quartet.
Only one way to get there,
says the silver-haired mother—
"I hope y'all out there are saved."
Everyone looks like they are saved
as they move their chairs to avoid the drips.

I deliver my speech about Pearl's
trailblazing dedication to justice
for women and civil rights and Asian orphans;
and her break with the Presbyterian mission board—
she wanted for all seekers
the privilege to discern
their own route to heaven.

A lady cutting the cake says "I have *The Pearl Buck Cookbook*."
Another says, "Pearl came to a picnic here once.
In her furs.
Drove off in a limousine.
She was nice. Told me the remembrance of this green valley
kept her going when she was afraid of the fires in the city."
We drink punch.
The sky clears.

Sydenstricker, Pearl's name,
is in my family.
An alcoholic hardware store owner married my aunt
over in Clifton Forge
forty miles from here,

Here, where they buried their hand-crafted clocks
in the good earth
when hungry soldiers rode through.
Here, in Pocahontas County,
where one generation
shows the next
how to carry on the music.

We disperse from the tent
as the sun sets.
I drive south
toward the lights of Lewisburg,
Pearl's good mud in my tires.

Returned from China, I Try to Find the Bar We Frequented

Driving through the neighborhood
where in college we had discovered
camaraderie of shared hope
and Taoist disavowal of war
(though we had not read the *Tao Te Ching*),
I cannot even find the street.
It was a tavern
on a green,
wasn't it?

We were halfway to dependency
upon escape
from an era that had broken
the Confucian pact:
"govern by moral force"
(though we had not read *The Analects*).

You laughed in your boat,
flunked out, and did all the paperwork
to become a conscientious objector
before your football player's
knees failed the physical.

Now, you have founded a company
that helps young people
recover from dependency
upon escape.

I want to visit you
now that we are old, traveled,
and done with indignation.

Do you still thrive in that town rejuvenated by artists?
Do you have children?
Do you still talk to mountains?
Do you offer jovial refreshment to fellow travelers from long ago?

Houseboat Conjuring

Chinese poets in their boats at night
wrote toward margins,
in fragile crafts,
moon and wine for light.
Often they capsized,
laughing,
at their drifting pages.

Why, amid all that fruitfulness—
hibiscus, lavender, iris, pistils of almond flowers, orchids—
did they write alone and drunk in their tiny boats?

Always the going away,
always the exile beyond understanding.

Li Bai leapt into the moon's reflection.

"Time of happiness
cannot be repeated," said Qu Yuan.

Oh let me try.

I bartered firewood for wine, and
after a night of chanting to the moon
with an old fisherman
on the first morning of spring,
I walked to my houseboat,
eager to revive
and write down
lost tales of
butterfly lovers,
the bridge of magpies,
mountain terrace tea gardens,
and the jade rabbit in the moon
so that I can see,
like those ducks diving in the reeds,
the flickering territory of dragons.

Day after Night on Black Mountain

I dropped Rick in Saluda
and headed back to Asheville
after a night under the dogwood moon,
when he told me how he holds on,
with a history
of his father, drunk, hammering birdhouses in the basement,
his sister, boxed-in in Charlotte, never recovered from
a visionary trip that ended in a fountain in Boston.

Our kinfolk insist that we document
every detour we took to get here.

He goes down to the Green River Tavern
and writes through the plane crash
that killed his brother in a tobacco field in 1969,
making a clearing,
with his pencil and a Sierra Nevada
as trucks with kayaks rattle by
in that sun on Sunday morning
after night on Black Mountain.

He says he wishes he had not
talked so much last night.

What have I ventured?
what have I laid bare?
Besides desire
to hear deep heart confessions launch.

To find a shape for his excursions,
he needs someone like me to hold them.
Mine, I clutch tight-fisted in my ribcage.

What a Dying College Cannot Take Down with It

I walk past the Humanities building,
abandoned first, when the sewer
backed-up into the halls;
dried paper shreds still speckle the hill.

Once girls choreographed poetry,
transforming homeless men
into a ballet of butterfly maidens
floating across a smoothed stage.

In the library, who will touch the books again?
No light and air on the pages of
Origin of Species or
Heraclitus' one-word aphorism "Akê,"

which means both silence and healing.
What can we hold on to in the fire of flux?
The grass greens
beside these locked buildings.

Earlier I drank a beer with Dave,
a photography professor unemployed,
at an outdoor café on State Street
near the Paramount Theater where Darrell Scott sang,

"You'll Never Leave Harlan Alive."
Dave has photographed edges of hard light
in empty parking lots
and taught firebuilding to Boy Scouts.

Will he leave Exit 7 alive?
Adapt or die. Evolution is not easy.
What can we retain while shadow
looms up the mountains?

The crooked road in southwest Virginia
passes through Dante, Bishop, Pound;
drugs pass hands
under town signs of dead poets.

While the school had an unpaid $13,000 light bill,
a photographer shot the geometry of vacancy,
a poet translated "I was drifting sand in the world's anger,"
a painter decorated magnolia leaves with birds,

like the sumi painters who found one hundred gradations
of black by varying the ink load
in their spare brushstrokes,
suggesting the kingfisher's knifelike dive.

West wind blows through the amphitheater
surrounded by rhododendron.
A skeleton crew sorts bankruptcy papers.
Blackbirds dart with twigs to a wobbly gutter.

Someone is mowing grass. The calligraphy of dogwoods
asks who should be forgiven. The old librarian,
who kept a key, enters the lightless library and feels
his way toward the shelf, "History: Lost Civilizations."

Not Lost: Island Voices

Down Uppowoc Street

Never stop listening to birds.
I glide through Old Town Manteo
on my bicycle.
Walter Raleigh left those colonists in 1585,
the year Shakespeare's children were baptized.

Shady houses, with windows open
and tomatoes ripening,
where lifesavers slept,
outliving shipwreck.

I am in no hurry,
holding on to this history of lostness.
You can only be lost if someone will grieve for you.

*

For Those in Peril on the Sea

Sailors know the hard language of knots,
fluent in dialect of butterfly and square.
In long-ago honeysuckle—
"how can we hear
its mirth and wisdom
while we are so preoccupied
with waiting for our captain's return?"
The bitter end
is the last part of a rope or chain, sailor.
Fear the yaw and love the moor.

*

Paradise Renovated

Four women with their yoga mats
stroll out of the high gates
of the Elizabethan Gardens
in the cool of the morning.
Precisely sculpted shrubbery
counterpoints the wilderness.

*The women of the Garden Club of North Carolina
have planted this garden in memory of the valiant men and women
who founded the first English colony in America.
From this hallowed ground on Roanoke Island
they walked away through the dark forest and into history.
1585-1951.*

Walk from the dark forest into
locked history.
Rise out of savasana,
and leave the key under the stone bench
outside the gate.

*

Homeless We Were, 1585

Walter Raleigh sailed out of these woods
leaving these sounds in the wind:
"He left us the cones, and we slept
where a little bit of boxwood stands now.
Lie down in the night needles;
shake off signs that we should abandon waiting."

International Architects, Cycling near Salzburg

We rode out of the city of salt
taking the tree-lined road to Hellbrunn
past nunnery, art studio, palace with grottoes for Neptune,
tractors gathering hay
until we wove into a forest and began to climb.

Kai, an Austrian architect,
showed us The Stone Theater, emerging
from a massive cave with seashells carved into the roof.
The first opera north of the Alps played here, Orfeo,
emerging from underworld, looking back.

Big shadows here at 47 degrees latitude,
damp cold coming off the rocks in June.
Suzanne whispered,
"I don't like it. Nazis hid here."
Kai said no, but Austrians had,
from air raids. "I was two.
My grandmother hugged me from the bombs."

As we pedaled the road
upon which Italian musicians had hauled the Renaissance northward,
I discussed built environments
with a man whom my countrymen had tried to kill.

We rode into the sun
and passed a zoo
where raw meat is catapulted
so cheetahs can accelerate
beneath the arc,
forgetting fences,
caught in the grace of survival.

Brickmaking, Chicago, 2016

The Galway Arms, in Lincoln Park—
the music there is true.
The bodhran player, his homeland
aglow in his heart, sings

of James Connolly, too weak to stand,
tied to a chair and shot
in the dust within the brick walls
of Kilmainham Gaol.

He sets down his drum and shouts to
a drunk DePaul student,
"This is a prayer, boy," and the pall
is upon us until

a lithe woman reverently enters
the circle and intones
"Even if they kill the men, they'll
know Irish aren't all gone."

What will you do with songs given
you? How bank against the
bitterness? Walking at midnight
along Clark Avenue,

I remember a man swinging
a scythe through his field of rye
on an Aran Island who hailed
the wandering lost me a

Gaelic salutation. Also
I evoke Martin L.
King, fifty years ago marching
toward a promised land

for his people to lay their heads.
Arm-in-arm with rabbi
and imam, he saw in Marquette
Park five thousand whites, gripped

by lost aspirations. Women
in pin curlers spit venom.
Lithuanians shouted,
"Go home," and King went down,

a brick to the back of his head,
solid in knowledge that
he was home among brick houses,
each brick cemented by

some displaced person's dream. Vacant
buildings around the park
today will not fall. Bricks, shaped from
earth and water, are fired

to build or break in the air. Bricks
are still made in the foundry
in Chicago. Moses' people
stamped bricks to build one more

civilization which thought it could
build its way beyond
its moment. Today, King's
brick memorial is ringed

by little mosaics of "home"
painted by Muslim kids,
Christian kids, and atheist kids—
a dialectic of

common desert ground.
Will you build or break
with the bricks of fortune
you have been handed?

Unwinding the Road

"How can you let it all go—
the armoire, the silver mint julep cups,
the Picasso print with his signature backwards,
this house, quiet in the trees?"
I ask her as we sit on her deck under pines.

She wants to go inside for air conditioning;
I hold out for summer dusk air
on a gravel road
two minutes from the subdivisions and Harris Teeters
of Providence Road.

"Debt," she says, "like a hyena panting
on my chest. I want to be free
for a while at the end
in a motor home, chugging along
where the sun leads.

"I have lost loves, dogs,
nursed my mother and father through cancers….
But if you know where they went,
they are not lost, right?
Why are there no paintings of Jesus laughing?"
as she looks at my Laughing Buddha beer bottle.

She offers me a pair of clogs,
 a dictionary, a Victorian print
we had found in a dumpster in Eugene.

Did you know when you were a little girl
that in spite of your generosity, your lovers
would fade away? Was it because the heart
space was too vast after the storms?

You arranged your own 40th birthday party
outside Hendersonville, NC.
I stopped at the cemetery on the way
to see the angel,
and then drove up to see women playing croquet
on a green plateau.
I told them Thomas Wolfe had the fire
so he could not fear the future because
"The last voyage, the longest, the best"
is the only adventure.

And soon, when you sell your house,
you will travel with your black lab—
like John Steinbeck—
and talk to retired couples
at a campground near Key Largo
about the time you dived
to the coral reefs
to seek the embrace of
Christ of the Abyss,
His arms stretching
toward the green surface of the bay.

Remember the times when hunger
for a home could be allayed
by a pot of fresh coffee percolating on a Coleman stove
on a picnic table
in the Deschutes,
a tent,
and a newspaper with classified ads
of boundless opportunities?

Why Don't You Stay, Just a Little Bit Longer?

> *You ask me why I dwell in the green*
> *mountain;*
> *I smile and make no reply*
> *for my heart is free of care.*
> *As the peach-blossom flows down stream*
> *and is gone into the unknown,*
> *I have a world apart that is not among men.*
> —Li Bai

I have been attracted to leaving—
those black and white cowboy movies,
townsfolk gazing from their motionless lives,
man on horseback trotting on.
I have left some interesting places
in Oregon and Florida
and welcomed going away parties.

We pulled out of Lexington, KY
in a U-Haul truck (with trailer)
and 2-month-old son
and in-migrated to Bluefield, WV.

And stayed.

You ask me why I live in blue mountains.
Ask my ancestors.

My mother grew up in the traintown of Clifton Forge.
Once she got out, she never wanted to go back.
When we passed through on a trip to Natural Bridge,
she scowled at a clapboard house on Alleghany Street.
Her sister's husband,
a distant cousin of Pearl Buck,
rocked on the porch of his hardware store
every afternoon, vodka in his coffee cup.

I remember feeling grave pull of
the mountains of boyhood beyond the piedmont.
You ask me why I live in blue mountains.
Ask the dead.

I met a man who taught
history and made his students enter maps
of the Mediterranean.
After nursing his mother through cancer,
he heard his diagnosis and shot himself in his snowy backyard.
I walk my dog past his grove every day,
blood still in the ground.

You ask me why I live in blue mountains.
Ask the abodes.

Spring strong under cold sun
orange on abandoned storefronts —
Rooms with a view on the edge
of an outpost,
love lost in the ruins,
tough answer for some mysteries.

You ask me why I live in blue mountains.
Ask the émigrés.

Crystal tried to hug her mother
who threw flowerpots on the kitchen floor,
then took her blue eyes
to Charleston, South Carolina,
and let her young, lived-before bones heal
in the salty sun.

My mother in 1928, smoking a cigarette,
shaved her legs in the Jackson River,
sixteen and knowing mountains sustain
the spirit of horizons.

You ask me why I live in blue mountains;
Ask the blossoms flowing down stream
gone into the unknown.

When I go out walkin' after midnight,
these mountains affirm
our rearranging of broken rocks,
and continue, calm and wise, when we turn out the lights.

Penelope's Eyes

Penelope sleeps alone a lot.
When he returns, she looks
out of the window
not at him, eager for his task of rebuilding
after the wreckage, the cave,
the glitter in faraway courtyards.

He had secreted the image of her green eyes
protected, undrowned, wrapped tight
in his depths as he sailed through other depths.
He had fallen eagerly into those eyes
on an unusually warm February
thirty-six years ago.
He did not even want to go to Troy;
hearth-tending had called him:
on upper floors,
boxes of hard-hearted manuscripts waiting for bonfires,
his father's broken valise, his grandfather's top hat
and rusted sword,
their daughter's paintings of benevolent wolves, ...

Solaces of return take time to unfold.
Much slaying of past selves to perform.
The security question is "What color are my eyes?"

He says, "I looked right through them one late afternoon
when the clouds shifted to make the ocean emerald,
your eyes the same hue, a jade gateway to harbors.
Once. when you mixed your water colors,
pushing the yellow ochre on your palette towards blue,
you caught the grey green glint of your own irises."

After a night of urgent storytelling,
they awoke to another gentle February,
clover and shamrocks hastening toward blossom,
newborn shoots spinning the colorwheel of the fields.
The hues of those eyes,
like the scar on his thigh,
reveal the escapades of homeplace.

You Live What the Birds Know

You have come to live
the way raptors ride the updrafts,
knowing deep in their little heartbeats
they must migrate to the tropical
upon a route etched upon their upbeat souls
in patterns of circumnavigation home.

Eagles, hawks, falcons
reach their destinations via acutest sensitivity
to the way air opens before them,
and you glide in that same wisdom.

Like the eagles
you make me want to brush the clouds
and touch you everywhere.

Birds sing in the morning
because light holds the key to celebration.

October afternoons ease their brilliance
into a warmth insignificant
without
the entire dark night we stared at wide-eyed,
me shivering
and you
reassuring as October
continuing.

You and I in a little space amid mountaintops
or on the streets encounter memos from those raptors
who direct us to
a café table in the Venice of our minds
full of birdsong
that we re-sing.

Floating Lanterns

Last night, I went to Cherokee Park
in Louisville and saw lanterns floating
on the pond for Hiroshima and Nagasaki.

A group of mostly old men and women sang
Donna nobis pacem, put candles into white paper bags
nailed to pieces of wood, and pushed them upon the waters.

A child stepped on a nail sticking from a boat
about to be launched. Her heel bled. Still not dark at 9:15.
Give us peace. Give us life after death.

A man in a canoe pulled the tiny barges of luminaries,
connected by string, into a rough circle.
Some sank; some drifted off in flames.

Like the Chinese poet who set his scroll and cups of wine
upon a floating tray and gently pushed them down the brook
through the garden to his lady bathing, I float this to you.

Now it is raining in the morning,
blue stillness over field descending to the lake
where water lilies crowd the shore.

You dwelled in what I imagined even before
I first saw you when you opened your door
to inarticulate men stamping their boots in the snow.

You are honeysuckle and spacious stories on a porch.
You are the clearing in the forest where sunrays break
into spokes, each one an arrow from the turning sky.

You were drawn to the stage, seduced by the way actors
create selves upon selves flowing one into the other
toward the open hearts of audiences.

You encountered the chronicle of that flow
one afternoon when you finished
War and Peace the week before our son was born.

"Vivid realism," Tolstoy said, reveals "inner continuity."
That is comforting. I usually rely upon metaphor:
the illusory immobility of sand dunes,

floating lanterns, starfish you see
awash upon the beach. I, eight hundred miles west,
on a path out of the basicilla into the woods

eye-to-eye with a deer
your sunset headed my way,
we both under the blue vault of heaven.

Separated we grow, making the vastness of the universe
less confounding. You expanded the range of what I feel.
No ascent without descent. The landscape is awash with stars.

In a letter, Vincent van Gogh sketched
a lamp post, twilight, a canal so that
he could give beauty to his brother.

Give. The landscape is awash with stars.
You do not like to wear shoes; you recognize,
like St. Francis in Bellini's painting of the ecstasy,

that we always walk on holy ground.
The landscape is awash with stars.
Swimming in the ocean with our daughter,

you dance a ballet dedicated to
the fluidity of experience.
You told me prayer is concentrated energy.

Like those lanterns floating into a rough circle of light—
some burned, some half-sunk and held by string—
you and I move together through a landscape awash with stars.

Robert Merritt grew up in Winston-Salem, North Carolina; attended the University of North Carolina and the University of Kentucky; and has lived in Bluefield, West Virginia, since 1990 with his wife, Mimi, and their two children. He is a Professor and Chair of the English Department at Bluefield College in the Blue Ridge Mountains of Virginia. He is former Dean of the College of Arts and Letters.

Merritt has taught American poetry and poetry writing at the Jiangsu Second Normal University in Nanjing, China, where he developed an affection for the people, the landscape, and the poetic traditions of China. He has tried to bring to his writing about the Appalachian Mountains the sense of geographical context of Chinese landscape painting in which humans appear inconsequential in relation to the trees, mountains, and rivers.

Merritt's interest in the Chinese literary tradition has led him to a renewed awareness of Pearl Buck, the author from a small town in Pocahontas County, West Virginia, who won the Pulitzer and Nobel prizes and is emerging as one of the few chroniclers in any language of Chinese working-class culture in the early twentieth century.

A member of the National Association for Poetry Therapy, he has worked to share and teach about the healing power of expressive writing.

Since 2012, he has been one of the fiction judges for the annual Lorian Hemingway Short Story Competition.

Merritt is the author of the poetry collections *The Language of Longing* and *Landscape Architects* and the critical book *Early Music and the Aesthetics of Ezra Pound*. His poetry and essays have appeared in *Kestrel, Pine Mountain Sand and Gravel, The Pikeville Review,* and *The Asheville Poetry Review,* among other journals, and the collections *The Southern Poetry Anthology, Vol. VII: North Carolina; Wild Sweet Notes II: Contemporary West Virginia Writers;* and *Coal: An Anthology.*

www.ingramcontent.com/pod-product-compliance
Lightning Source LLC
LaVergne TN
LVHW041504070426
835507LV00012B/1326